How to P

Easily for Beginners

Step-by-Step

Comprehensive Blueprint to

Picking Locks for Beginners

Introduction

Imagine coming back home after a very long and crazy day, tired and only desiring to get home and lay your head to rest. But on reaching home, tired as you are, you realize your key is missing. You check all your pockets and any likely place you could put it, but you don't find it. You lost the key.

What next? Finding a locksmith would take forever, and breaking in is not an ideal option. You're left with either finding a hotel room, spending the night at your friend's place, or asking your neighbor to host you. This is when you wish you knew how to pick locks.

If you've ever gone through this, I believe you loathed the experience and would not want to go through it a second time. This is where learning to pick locks can be an invaluable skill that you can also use to help your loved ones out when they find themselves in such a predicament or, better still, earn something from it as a professional locksmith.

Now, if you want to learn about lock picking and have questions such as:

Can anyone pick locks?

How can I pick various types of locks?

What tools do I need to pick a lock?

...then read on, as this book will answer all the above questions and teach you everything you need to know about picking locks, from the tools you need, the different types of locks you can pick, which are the simplest and most complex locks to pick, and so much more!

Let's get started!

PS: I'd like your feedback. If you are happy with this book, please leave a review on Amazon.

Please leave a review for this book on Amazon by visiting the page below:

https://amzn.to/2VMR5qr

Table of Contents

Chapter 1: The Parts of a Door Lock

Lock picking is simply opening a lock without using the key. It is the art of manipulating the components of a lock to open it without damaging the lock or its door. Before we look at how you can pick the different locks, let us first look at the various parts of a lock so that you can understand the specific parts you will be manipulating.

It is essential to note that there are various types of locks, which means they have different parts. However, the following are the standard and vital parts of all locks:

1. The cylinder

2. The strike plate

3. The bolt

Keyway

Cylinder

Knob

Bolts

Strike Plate

¹Figure 1 image credit iStock

1. The Cylinder

The cylinder is the main body of a lock and contains the locking mechanism. It can also be referred to as the lock body, shell, or housing. The cylinder is where you slide in your key. It has springs with pins that open or lock the lock.

When you insert a key, the pins do not turn unless the key pushes them in the right direction/right pattern, which only the correct key of the lock can do.

2. The Bolt

The bolt is the metallic part of the lock that protrudes from the door into the door frame to lock the door. When a door is

7

closed, it stretches into the door frame and holds the door from being open.

There are various types of bolts depending on the type of lock.

The standard bolts are:

- **Spring bolt**

Also known as the latch bolt, the spring bolt is always held in place by a spring. To open the door, you compress the spring by pulling the bolt to detach the door from the frame. When the spring is released, it pushes the bolt back into the door frame to close the door.

[2]Figure 2 image credit Shutterstock

- **Deadbolt**

As opposed to the spring bolt, the deadbolt does not use springs and is more secure than the spring bolt and the others.

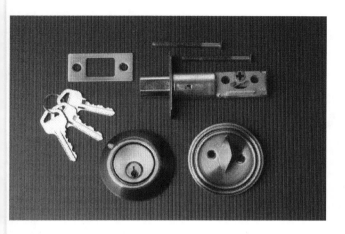

3Figure 3 image credit iStock

- **The barrel bolt**

These are bolts that are held by long metallic cylinders. These locks are ideal for internal doors. To lock a door with a barrel bolt, you only need to push the bolt into the matching hole/cavity into the door frame, and to open it, pull the bolt out from the door frame using your thumb.

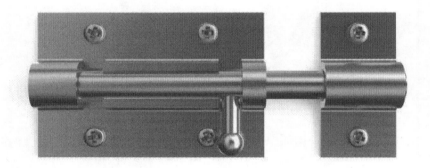

4Figure 4 image credit Shutterstock

The Strike Plate

This is the metallic plate fixed on the door frame at the same level as the door lock. This plate contains the cavity or the hole in which the bolt stretches into the door frame to lock it.

5Figure 5 image credit Shutterstock

3. The Handle

The handle, also called the knob, is an external part of a lock, which (in spring bolt locks) you twist or push downwards to open the door.

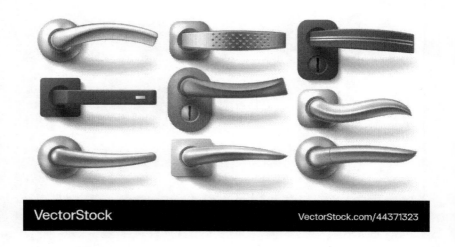

VectorStock   VectorStock.com/44371323

[6] Figure 6 image credit Vectorstock

Not all door handles are twisted or pulled down to open the door; other handles are for pushing or pulling the door open.

4. The Box

This is the hole held by the strike plate on the door frame. It is into the box that the bolt extends to the door frame to lock a door.

5. Keyway

This is the opening into which you insert the key into the lock's cylinder.

6. Cam

It is a cylindrical body that stretches into the lock. It is the part that allows the bolt to slide across to the door frame to close the door.

7. Rotor

We find a rotor within the cylinder. When you turn the cylinder to unlock the door, it hits the rotor, which releases the bolts to open the lock.

8. Cotter pin

The cotter pin allows the rotor turn to open or close the door when you insert the key.

9. Spring

Springs hold the lock pins in place and also enable the pins to move up and down swiftly.

Let's now look at the tools you will need to use when lock picking.

Chapter 2: Tools for Picking Locks

There are various tools used in picking locks, and they vary depending on the lock you will be picking. Let's start with the tools for picking standard locks, which are the most common ones.

1. Hook

Hooks are narrow and pointy picking tools that are used to pinpoint and reach the pins within the cylinder. These tools are ideal for picking single-pin locks, as they can locate and manipulate a single pin at a time.

7**Figure 7 image credit Shutterstock**

There are various types of hooks depending on their length and shape. For example, short hooks, long hooks, gonzo hooks, and Gem hooks.

- **Short Hook**

Short hooks are primarily used to pick tumbler locks. They pick a pin at a time.

14

- **Long Hooks**

Long hooks are used to pick locks with a larger tumbler.

2. Gem

[8]Figure 8 Image Credit Shutterstock

The gem has a slight difference from the hook at the tip. It has an extended tip making it ideal when picking waded locks, locks with radical biting, or locks with paracentric keyways.

3. Diamond Picks

Like the hook, diamond picks are ideal for single-pin picking but can also work in other lock-picking techniques, as we shall see. You can easily distinguish them by their triangular shape at the tip.

We have the Full Diamond pick and the Half Diamond picks.

- **Half Diamond Pick**

⁹**Figure 9 Image Credit Shutterstock**

Half diamond pick is a combination of the short standard hook and the Gem. The small half-diamond is ideal for single-pin picking, while we can use the large half-diamond pick in single-pin lock picking and other techniques of picking locks.

- **Full Diamond pick**

This hook has a diamond shape at the tip. It is used to pick single-pin locks or manipulate a single pin at a time, but it can also help open multi-barrel locks. Full-diamond picks are not as common as the half-diamond pick.

4. Rakes

¹⁰**Figure 10 Image Credit Shutterstock**

A rake is a pick with a serrated edge. As opposed to the hook, which picks one pin at a time, rakes are used to manipulate multiple pins simultaneously. This is called raking.

Rakes help pick locks faster than the hook and the diamond.

There are several types of rakes. For example:

- **The city rake**

This rake resembles a saw in design. It has teeth(rakes) that generate more movements than the hook or diamond, hence can quickly manipulate several pins.

[11]Figure 11 Image Credit Imagefx

- **Snake Rake**

As the name suggests, snake rakes are curvy in form.

[12]Figure 12 Image Credit Imagefx

5. The tension wrench

Tension wrenches will help you create bidding pins by applying pressure to the lock's plug. This tool is among the basic tools you will need as a picker. The tool helps you hold the picked pins in place as you turn the plug to open the lock.

18

[13]Figure 13 image credit Shutterstock

Ball picks

Ball picks are used to pick disc tumblers and wafer locks since they can adjust the individual disc or wafer in any direction. Their circular tip distinguishes them.

For ball picks, we have snowman (double ball pick), half snowman (double half-ball pick), the ball pick, and the half ball pick.

[14]Figure 14 Image Credit Shutterstock

6. Pick Guns

Lock-picking guns are advanced tools that are used to force a lock to open faster without a key. Pick guns involve inserting a thin pin into the lock, then the gun simultaneously fires the rod against the lock pins to free the cylinder.

Lock-picking guns feature various pick heads that get connected to the gun section. We have two types of pick guns; the electric pick gun and the manual pick gun.

[15]**Figure 15 image credit Shutterstock**

- **The manual lock pick gun**

Lock pick guns apply the law of transfer of energy in physics, hence are not a trial-and-error method as the traditional picks.

How a pick gun works:

Insert the thin rod attached to the gun into the lock through the keyway, and fire the gun. The rod inside the lock will then push against the lock pins to free the cylinder. This will make it possible to turn the cylinder and open the lock.

Since the guns are not a trial-and-error tool, they help open locks quickly. However, they may damage your lock to the extent of rendering the original key to the lock useless.

- **The electric pick gun**

Electric gun picks use a motor or electromagnet to vibrate the thin rod or the needle inserted into the lock. When you insert the needle to fit under the key pins, pull the trigger, and the motor will vibrate the needle at a frequency that will manipulate the pins, allowing you to turn the plug.

In as much as the electric guns are fast, they are not ideal for all locks, especially the complicated ones. This is because complex locks easily break when much force is used to pick them. So, these guns are mostly suitable for use on simple locks.

7. Try out keys

Try-out keys are the ones we popularly know as 'master keys.' These stainless steel keys come in a set of different sizes for the different keyway sizes. They resemble the normal lock keys, only that they do not have the unique design for a single lock.

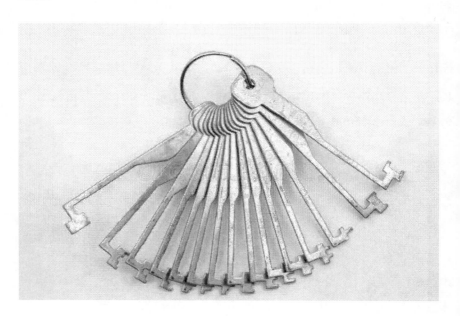

[16]**Figure 16 image Dreamstime**

8. Tubular lock pick

This pick is for picking locks with round keyways. It is the perfect tool for picking radial pin tumbler locks.

9. Shim

Shim is a thin metallic tool used to pick locks with shackles.

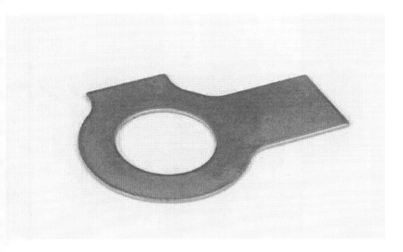

[17] **Figure 17 image credit Shutterstock**

10.   DIY Lock Pick From a Paper Clip

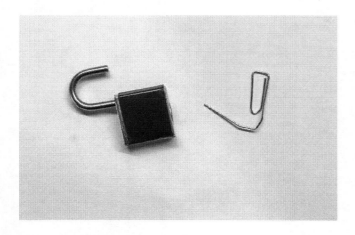

¹⁸**Figure 18 image credit iStock**

Did you know that you can make your own lock-picking tool?

Have two metallic paper clips which are at least 4cm long. This is to ensure that the pick will be long enough to reach the interior of a lock.

- Straighten the outer bend of one paper clip to get one straight end, and the other end should be curved

- Twist the curved end to hold on the straight side to form a handle,

- Using pliers, bend the tip of the straight end to create bumps (M-shaped bend)

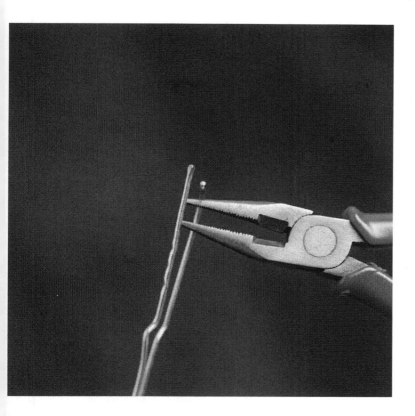

¹⁹Figure 19 Image Credit Imagefx

- Use the second pin to make a tension wrench. Unfold the ends and straighten them to give you two parallel sides.

- Flatten the u-bend to bring the two parallel sides into contact with each other and twist the ends against each other.

- Bend the pin into an L shape to give you the tension wrench

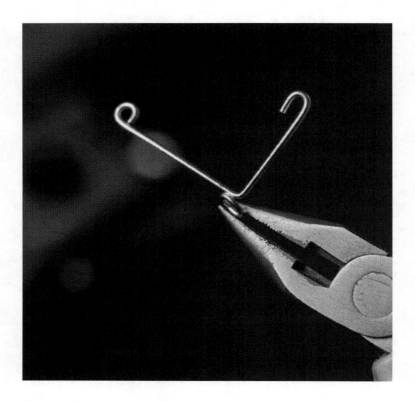

[20]**Figure 20 Image Credit Imagefx**

What to Consider when Buying Lock Picking Tools

The market is flooded with these tools; the same tool, the same size, but different quality. As you set out to buy your set of tools, it is crucial to consider the following factors;

1. Quality of the pick

The quality of the pick will be determined by the material used to make it. A good quality tool will last longer and enable you to realize the value of the money you spend to buy them. Stainless steel tools are of good quality as they are more resistant to corrosion and rusting and hence last longer.

2. Fineness

The height and thickness of the blade measure the fineness of a pick.

The thickness of a good blade should be between 0.5mm and 0.8mm. Blades below 0.5mm don't have much strength, hence can bend or break while in use, while thicker than 0.8mm will not fit into many keyholes.

The height of the pick blade is also essential to check for fitting purposes. A standard lock pick is 5/16 inches in height, which should easily fit most locks.

3. Usability/Utility

This is the ability of the pick to serve the purpose for which you are buying it. Picks that you can improvise easily to pick other locks, other than the specific ones they pick best, have higher utility than those you cannot improvise.

Other factors to consider are the price, the locks to pick, and whether the picks are for commercial use.

Code of Conduct

Most people shy away from lock picking with the belief that this is a criminal activity. This is because criminals, especially thieves, always use this skill to break into other people's homes. But just as not all IT gurus are hackers, not all who can pick locks are criminals. Lock-picking is a beneficial skill that a decent person can learn and be of great help to themselves and even to others.

The following are the two simple principles that should guide you:

1. **Only pick locks that belong to you**

2. **If need be, only pick a lock that the owner permits you**

Since you are now acquainted with the parts of a lock and the tools for picking a lock, we can now get started with the lock-picking techniques before we get to various types of locks and how to pick them.

Chapter 3: Lock-Picking Techniques

As we get into the practical aspects of lock picking, various techniques exist. Listed below are some of these techniques:

- Single pin picking

- Raking

- Using pick guns

- Picking combination locks

- Picking locks with security pins

These are just but a few techniques. There are many more, like scrubbing, bypassing, shimming, etc.

Single Pin Picking

Single-pin picking (SPP) is the most basic technique for picking locks. It is among the most reliable techniques, as you will be picking the pins one at a time.

In as much as SPP is not the fastest technique, it is a very reliable technique and ideal for beginners. This technique is suitable for picking pin tumbler locks, though you can also apply it to pick other types of locks.

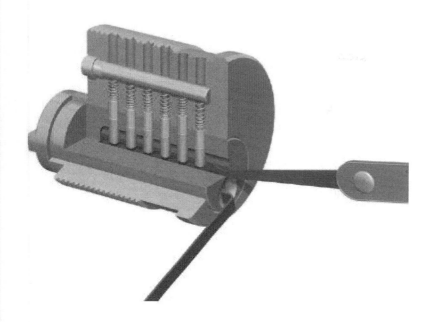

[21]Figure 21 image credit Alamy

How to use single-pin picking

In our case here, we will use a tension wrench and a hook to pick a pin-tumbler lock.

1. Use a tension wrench to form the initial binding pin

Insert the tension wrench into the base of the keyway. The tension wrench will provide the force required to turn the plug and create a binding pin.

31

Maintain the pressure you apply on the tension wrench throughout the picking process. This means you keep holding the tension wrench throughout and never let go to maintain the force.

2. Locate the initial binding pin

Note: A binding pin usually holds more pressure than the other pins. This means as you try the various pins, the binding pin will feel stiffer to lift than the others.

Insert your hook into the keyway and locate the pins. Try lifting each pin by simply tilting the hook upwards to find the harder/stiffer pin to lift.

3. Set the initial binding pin by lifting it

After locating the initial binding pin, lift it using the hook until you hear a click or until it does not feel stiff anymore. The click, which is audible, signifies that you have successfully set the binding pin.

4. Locate the second binding pin and set

After setting the initial pin, try the remaining pins again to identify the second binding pin. The second binding pin will be stiffer this time, the same as the subsequent binding pins.

Once you locate the second binding pin, lift it until you set it, just as the initial binding pin.

5. Repeat the procedure for the subsequent binding pins and set

Locate the next binding pin using the same method above and set. Repeat this procedure until you successfully set all the pins.

6. Turn the plug to open the lock

Once you have set all the pins, there will be no hindrance to the shear line for the plug to rotate. Fully rotate the plug to disengage the lock.

And congratulations, you have successfully picked your first lock!

NOTE: If you are not able to locate any binding pin, there is a possibility that you have either:

- Not applied enough pressure using your tension wrench, or

- You have over-set or under-set a pin.

For case one, try to apply more pressure using the tension wrench, and for the second case, loosen the tension wrench, allow all the pins to drop, and start the process again.

33

Raking

As opposed to single-pin picking, which we just learned, raking is much faster. In single-pin picking, we located and set the binding pins sequentially, one after the other. Here, we will set several pins at once, making raking a much faster method to pick a lock.

Raking is ideal for picking pin tumbler locks and wafer locks. However, it is ineffective for picking locks with extra security properties, like sidebars and security pins.

This technique is also very unpredictable and can damage your lock if you do not use it appropriately.

There are various raking styles, including scrubbing, rocking, and zipping. Let us start with scrubbing:

1. Scrubbing

Just as the name suggests, this racking style uses a rake to scrub on the pins at a considerable speed to open the lock. The scrubbing is more like how you brush your teeth.

Below are simplified steps for you to rake a lock successfully;

Tools: tension wrench and a rake

- ***Create a binding pin***

Similar to single-pin picking, the first step is to make a binding pin by creating tension into the lock using a tension wrench. Ensure that you maintain the pressure as you rake.

- ***Insert the rake into the keyway and start scrubbing***

Having created the binding pin, insert the rake into the keyway to the end, then lift the rake a bit to press the pins. Scrub the pins by moving the rake in and out at a reasonable speed as you would brush your teeth.

As you scrub, keep adjusting the angle of the rake, speed, and height. If you do this correctly, the lock will unlock in less than ten seconds.

A tension wrench is vital in raking, so ensure that you have the most appropriate one for the lock you are picking. If the lock fails to unlock, withdraw the rake and the tension wrench and start again. If it still doesn't unlock, you may need to change your tension wrench to a lighter or a heavier one.

NOTE: Ensure you are not rough with your scrubbing, as it can damage your lock.

Tips for successful raking

Raking has a lower success rate compared to single-pin picking. For you to achieve a higher rate of success in raking, the following tips will be beneficial:

Single pin pick: If you have tried several times and realize that you have not set all the pins and that they aren't positively responding anymore, you can single-pick the remaining pins using your rake.

Listen to feedback: Always be keen to listen to the feedback as you rake. Try different rakes, tension wrenches, and even different locks to feel the feedback. This will help you know if the process is successful.

Pulsing: Gently apply pressure to the tension wrench when raking. Gentle pressure works much better than pressing on the tension wrench.

Using a Pick Gun

Using pick guns is very suitable for picking pin tumbler locks. As much as it is faster than any other technique, pick guns do not work well with all locks. Wafer locks, locks with serrated pins, and locks with counter-drilled pins are some of the locks that pick guns are not very effective on.

As we learned earlier, there are two types of pick guns; Electric pick guns and manual pick guns.

Let us learn how you will pick locks using each of these pick guns:

1. Manual pick

Tools: a pick gun, needles, and a tension wrench

Pick guns always come with different needles that work as the picks. Therefore, do not worry about the pins.

The following steps guide you as you use your manual pick gun:

- *Install a needle on the pick gun*

Select one pin, slide it into the needle slot, and tighten it firmly on the gun. Once you have installed the needle, your gun will be ready for use.

- *Insert the tension wrench into the keyway of your lock*

As we learned earlier, slide in your tension wrench at the base of the keyway, slightly applying tension using the tension wrench to create a binding pin.

- ### *Insert the installed needle into the keyway*

Maintaining the pressure on the wrench, pick the gun on which you installed the needle. Slide the needle into the keyway until you can feel the arrangement of the pins and resistance of the plug.

- ### *Fire the gun*

Once the needle is inside the lock to the point you feel the resistance of the plug, pull the trigger. When you do this, the hummer inside the gun will release, forcing the needle to bump upwards to push the pins against the springs to the sheer line.

- ### *Adjust the intensity*

Most pick guns have a thumbwheel that you can use to adjust the intensity of the gun. As you start the picking, ensure that you start with the low-intensity setting, then adjust bit by bit as you continue until the lock gets unlocked.

If your lock does not open after several attempts, get back to your tension wrench and apply a little more tension to it. Repeat the process.

2. Electric pick gun

An electric pick gun, abbreviated as EPG, is an upgraded manual pick gun. As we learned earlier and as the name suggests, electric guns use electromagnetism or a motor to vibrate the needle.

Where there is a need for speed, an electric pick gun becomes the tool of choice to pick your lock. This is because it is much faster than any other tool and has a higher success rate than the manual pick gun.

Let's get to know how to use this electric pick gun;

- ***Ensure that the gun has enough power***

Since this is an electric gadget, always ensure that it is fully charged because it will be useless if it does not have power.

- **Install the needle**

After confirming that your gun has some charge, select the needle that will be ideal for the lock you are picking, then attach it to the tip of the gun (the designated tip). Ensure that you fix your needle and tighten it correctly.

- ***Tension wrench***

Insert your tension wrench into the base of the keyway and apply a little tension on the wrench to create the binding pin.

- ***Insert the gun pin into the lock***

Insert the needle attached to your gun into the lock through the keyway until you feel the pins' arrangements and the plug's resistance.

- **Pull the trigger**

Once the needle is inside the lock, as you maintain the pressure on the tension wrench, pull the trigger. The motor/electromagnets in the gun will vibrate the needle, making it push the lock pins as it resets them. Once you set the pins, the lock will unlock.

This process should take the shortest time possible - less than ten seconds. If your lock doesn't unlock, try more but gentle pressure on the tension wrench or add a little more pressure on it as you lift your needle a little higher.

When you do everything right, the lock will unlock within no time.

As you use the EPG, note the following;

- Do not extendedly pull the trigger, as continuous action can damage the motor of your gun

- Pull the trigger as you let go at an interval of not more than two seconds since continuous vibration will not work.

Bypassing

To improve the locks' security, manufacturers have devised ways to make their locks resistant to picking. Most locks today have anti-picking pins, making picking them very challenging. Here, we will learn how to bypass the security pins/anti-picking pins:

The anti-picking pins

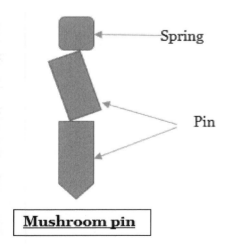

Spring

Pin

Mushroom pin

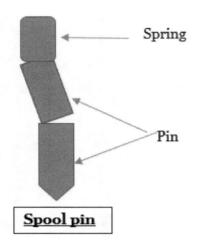

Spring

Pin

Spool pin

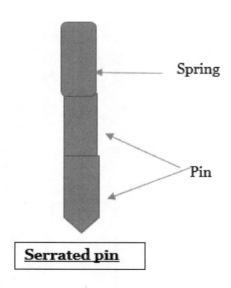

Spring

Pin

Serrated pin

Anti-picking pins are placed between the lock pins and the spring. They take different shapes, allowing them to manipulate the picking process by giving you wrong feedback.

When you insert your tension wrench and apply tension to the plug, the anti-picking pin will slightly bend, as you can see in the diagram above, giving a small allowance for you to turn the plug slightly, not fully, to unlock the lock.

The slight turn the security pin allows makes you think you have picked the lock successfully. This misleading feedback makes picking locks with security pins very challenging.

How to bypass the anti-picking pins/ security pins

As shown in the diagram above, when you apply tension to the plug, the pins bend, allowing the plug to make a slight turn. The security pins then become depressed or stuck. To bypass this, you must reapply some tension on your plug.

Then the pins will counterturn to the locking direction. This process may seem easy on paper, but practically very challenging. Bypassing will therefore involve a lot of mastery and practice until you get it right.

The following steps will help you to bypass the security pins successfully:

Tools*:* tension wrench and a half diamond

- Insert the tension wrench into the base of the keyway. This first tension will make the security pins tilt a bit, allowing the plug to turn and the pins to get depressed.

- Vary the tension you put on your wrench until the plug counter rotates back to the locking position. This will make the security pins align with the shear line again. Since the security pins were depressed, the depressing force will push them above the shear line once they align with the shear line.

- Note that as you vary the tension, the pick, which we picked a half diamond in this case, is also in use trying to push up the lock pins.

- Once the security pins move above the shear line, you will then freely push the lock pins upwards.

As we learned earlier in single-pin picking, you will know that you have set a pin successfully when you push it upward and get an audible click.

Jiggling

Jiggling is a technique that probably everyone has applied with or without knowing. We do this most of the time with our locks. As the name suggests, jiggling involves making various moves in your padlock using a key to reset the pins.

To simplify this, let me give you a much more familiar instance you might have used this technique or seen someone use it.

Jiggling is what you do when your lock sometimes refuses to respond positively to its key. When you insert your correct key, and the lock doesn't unlock, you will try to move the key severally, applying a little more force. You will move your key up, down, side by side, a bit out, and in until the lock unlocks. This is jiggling.

If you have lost the right key, you will need to find a key that fits into your lock well and try to unlock it by moving it severally until it unlocks. If the key you selected did not open the lock after the jiggling, try another key that fits until it works out.

With these basic techniques, you can start practicing picking different types of locks.

Chapter 4: Picking Different Types of Locks

Now that you have learned the parts of a lock, the tools for picking a lock, and the techniques you will apply, you are ready to pick!

Understanding the locks you will pick much deeper is vital so you know which technique works better for each lock.

Here are the types of locks, how they work, and how to pick each of them;

Pin Tumbler Locks

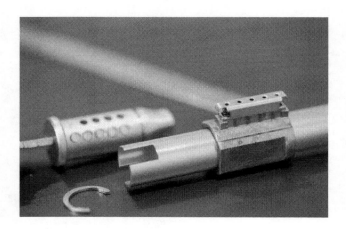

[22]Figure 22 image credit Stock Adobe

These are locks that make use of pins with altered lengths to lock.

46

CYLINDER PIN-TUMBLER LOCK

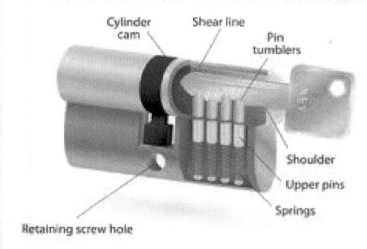

Cylinder cam
Shear line
Pin tumblers
Shoulder
Upper pins
Springs
Retaining screw hole

23Figure 23 Image Credit Shutterstock

There are two types of pin tumbler locks:

In-line tumbler lock: These pin tumblers have pins arranged in a line, as in the image above. They use flat keys to open.

47

²⁴Figure 24 image credit iStock

Radial pin tumbler locks: These locks have pins arranged circularly around the plug. They use round keys to open.

48

How a pin tumbler works

Pin tumbler locks have a sequence of pins; the key pins are also called upper pins, and the driver pins are also known as the pin tumblers. These pins are always pushed upwards (according to the image above) and held in place by the springs, making them not align correctly with the shear line. When the pins do not align with the shear line, the cylinder cannot turn, keeping the lock closed.

When you insert the correct key, the pins will push downwards to align with the shear line, making it possible to turn the cylinder to open the lock.

When you use the wrong key, the pins will not turn; hence the cylinder will not turn to open the door.

Pin tumblers are mainly used on doors, vending machines, bicycle locks, cabinets, drawers, game machines, and padlocks.

- ### *The tubular lock pick*

The tubular lock pick is made in such a way that it is very reliable for picking radial locks. The nature of the tubular pick makes it require minimum effort and takes the least

49

time to pick a radial lock. This tool also has a high rate of success.

This tubular lock pick has a tube-like metal attached to the handle. The metal fits the keyway of a radial pin tumbler lock. The metallic tube has needles, also known as pick wires, that you can adjust by protruding or retracting them and a threaded bolt to tighten or loosen the needles.

How to Pick Pin Tumbler Locks

The most appropriate way to pick these locks is using the raking technique, single pin picking, a pick gun, and tubular picks for the radial pin tumbler.

Your knowledge of raking, picking single pins, and using a pick gun will make this easier. Raking and pick guns may not work for radial pin tumbler locks, so we will learn how to pick them using a tubular pick. You can also pick radial pin tumbler locks by single picking them.

Padlocks

Padlocks are portable types of locks that are not fixed on a door. They use shackles to secure an item.

[26]**Figure 26 image credit iStock**

A wide range of padlocks vary in sizes, styles, and even brands, but we categorize all as either keyed padlocks or combination padlocks.

Both padlocks have the following standard components;

- The shackle

- Locking mechanism

- The body

1. Keyed Padlocks

Keyed padlocks are the most common locks and use keys to lock or unlock. These padlocks are either key-retaining (you cannot withdraw the key from the lock when it is unlocked) or non-key-retaining (you can remove the key from the padlock even when it is unlocked.)

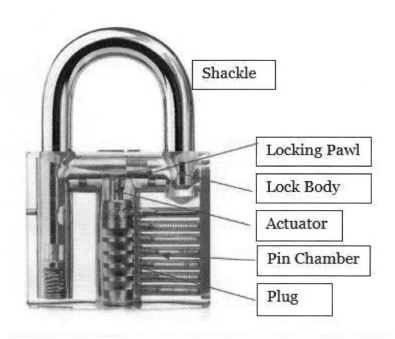

Shackle

Locking Pawl

Lock Body

Actuator

Pin Chamber

Plug

[27]**Figure 27 image credit Dreamstime**

- ***How padlocks work***

When you insert the right key into the lock through the keyhole, the key pins will move up and down to align with the sheer line. This will enable the plug to turn.

When the plug turns, it will move the actuator with it, pulling the locking pawl out of the notch on the shackle. The shackle will release and be pushed outwards by a spring to open.

The following are the types of padlocks:

- *Waterproof padlocks*: These padlocks are ideal for outdoor security. Non-corrosive materials (mostly plastic or rubber) cover them, making them withstand harsh weather.

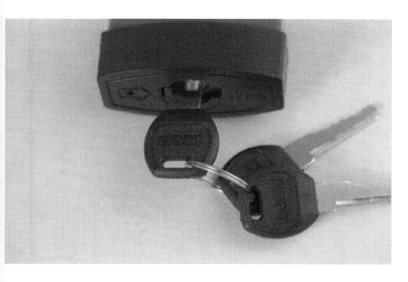

[28]**Figure 28 image credit Shutterstock**

- *Closed shackle padlock:* They have long shoulders to cover the shackle.

²⁹Figure 29 image credit Dreamstime

- *Long shackle padlocks:* These padlocks are ideal for attaching things that are distant apart.

³⁰Figure 30 image credit Dreamstime

- *Discus padlocks:* These padlocks are round and have their shackle closed.

2. Combination padlock

Combination locks use codes to open.

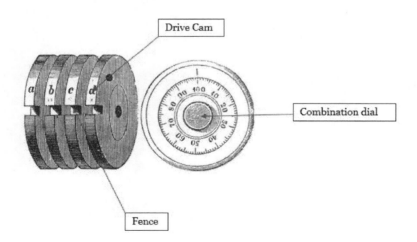

- ## *How Combination padlocks work*

These locks have a combination dial attached to the spindle in the lock. The spindle extends inwards through the cam and several wheels.

When you enter the correct code, the spindle will turn the drive cam attached to the drive pins. The drive pin then spins the first wheel attached to it, turning the next wheel to the next and the next to the last. The wheels have notches that will align, releasing the shackles to open the lock.

There are several types of combination locks, which include dial combination padlocks, scrolling combination padlocks, luggage padlocks, key-controlled scrolling combination padlocks, and key-controlled dial combination padlocks. We shall summarize all these types into two categories: single-rotating dials and multiple-dial locks.

- ## *Single rotating dial*

The single-rotating dial is very common in safes, lockers, and padlocks. These locks provide mid-level to high levels of security, hence very common.

33Figure 33 image credit Shutterstock

• *How to crack a single dial combination lock*

Cracking these locks' codes will not be as easy as the multiple-dial combination locks you'll pick next.

These locks have combinations that can go up to over 60,000 combinations. With such combinations, it is evident that cracking these codes can take you an eternity.

To crack these kinds of locks, the model of the lock you are picking is critical. Find out the model from the lock's serial number (which is indicated on every lock). Note this serial number down.

Below is the step-by-step procedure to follow:-

- Set a common starting point

After noting down the lock's serial number, you will have to clear the lock by setting a common starting point. To do this, rotate the dial clockwise past the zero mark at least three times; ensure that your rotations go past the zero mark three times or more and stop the last spin at the zero mark.

- Put some tension on the shackle

Here, you can use your index finger to pull it up or use a rope to tie the shackle, attach it to a firm object, and then pull the lock. Don't apply much pressure, as too much pressure will make it impossible to turn the dial. Also, don't apply too little pressure, as this will make the dial turn freely, making the process ineffective.

- Find the sticking range

Maintaining the gentle pressure on the shackle, rotate the dial in the anticlockwise direction until you reach the point where the dial moves freely and gets stuck. Note down the number on which the dial got stuck (for example, let's say your dial stopped at number 7.5).

Then, rotate the dial in the clockwise direction without letting go of the pressure on the shackle to the point where the dial no longer moves. Note the number at which your dial stopped in the clockwise direction. (For example, say the dial stopped at number 5.5). The sticking range is, therefore (5.5, 7.5).

NOTE: If the dial remains stuck at point zero as you start your initial rotation, let go of the pressure on the shackle and rotate the dial slightly to one or two numbers ahead of zero. Then apply the pressure on the shackle again and continue with the rotation.

- Determine the sticking point

After we have found the sticking range, we determine the sticking point, which is the number between the two sticking range numbers. For example, in our case, since we have 5 and 7, the number between them, which is 6, becomes the sticking point.

If you get a range of (3, 5), the sticking point becomes 4; if (5.5, 7.5), the sticking point is 6.5.

- Find the second sticking range and sticking point

After finding the first sticking range and sticking point, you will need to reset the lock to a starting point before starting to find the second sticking range and sticking point. To reset the lock, rotate the dial in the anticlockwise direction until you pass the highest number in the sticking range by one.

For example, in our case, the dial stopped at the number 7 during the first anticlockwise rotation. At the moment, our dial is pointing at 5. Rotate back in an anticlockwise direction to point 7+1=8. Point 8 is our new starting point.

After resetting the dial to this new starting point 8, apply the pressure on the shackle again and rotate the dial anticlockwise to the point the dial will not move anymore. Note down the new anticlockwise stopping point (for example, 11), then rotate the dial back in the clockwise direction to where it will stop. Note down this new number, say 9. The second range, therefore, is (11, 9). This range gives us 10 as the second sticking point.

- Find subsequent sticking range and sticking points

Reset the lock by rotating it anticlockwise past the highest number of the range by one. For example, to find the third range, rotate the dial anticlockwise to 11+1=12. You will always use the previous range to reset the lock for the next range.

After resetting, rotate the dial anticlockwise until the dial stops, note the number, then rotate back clockwise until the dial stops. Note this number. The two numbers give us the next range. Reset and repeat until you get ten sticking points.

NOTE: Reset the lock after each sticking range.

The table below shows an example of sticking ranges and sticking points.

Sticking range	Sticking point
(7.5, 5.5)	6.5
(11,9)	10
(14.5, 12.5)	13.5
(17.5, 15.5)	16.5
(21, 19)	20
(26.5, 24.5)	25.5
(28, 26)	27
(31, 29)	30
(34.5, 32.5)	33.5
(37.5, 35.5)	36.5
(39, 0)	0

- Determine the third combination number

Using examples in the table above, let's find the third combination number from which we can determine the rest of the numbers. Our table has the sticking points in fractions and whole numbers. Work with the whole numbers and drop all the fractions. We now have 0, 10, 20, 27, and 30.

Pick the odd one out of the remaining numbers and use it as the third combination number. In our case here, 27 is the odd one since it doesn't end with a zero. 27 now becomes our third combination number.

- Determine the first and second combination number

To find the first combination number, we will have to find the ten possibilities of this first number.

Take the third combination number, which is 27, and divide it by 4.

(27/4) = 6 remainder 3. Take note of the remainder; in our case is 3.

Let's now find the 10 possibilities of the first number. To achieve this, we will apply the arithmetic sequence formula using 4 and the 3 that remained to get the ten possibilities of the first combination number.

3

3+4=7,

7+4=11,

11+4=15,

15+4=19,

19+4=23,

23+4=27,

27+4=31,

31+4=35,

35+4=39

These make our ten possibilities of the first combination number.

For the second combination number, we again determine the 10 possibilities. Here, we will subtract 2 from 3 that remained. We remove 2 because we are looking for the second combination number.

Note that if you did everything right in this process, you should always have 0, 1, 2, and 3 as your remainders.

Anything beyond 3 is an indication that something is not right.

As you find the second combination number possibilities, if your remainder is 0, or 1, you will add 2 instead of subtracting. Only subtract when the remainder is either 2 or 3.

In our case, the remainder was 3, so we will subtract 2 to give us the first possible number, then add 4 sequentially to provide us with the subsequent possibilities up to the 10th one.

3-2=1

1+4=5

5+4=9

9+4=13

13+4=17

17+4=21

21+4=25

25+4=29

29+4=33

33+4=37

This will give us 1, 5, 9, 13, 17, 21, 25, 29, 33 and 37.

We then narrow this down by eliminating the two numbers adjacent to our third combination (27). In this case, we will eliminate 25 and 29 to leave us with 8 possibilities; 1, 5, 9, 13, 17, 21, 33, and 37.

Having found the ten possible first numbers, the eight possible second numbers, and our by default third number, we now form the possible combinations. For example: (3, 1, 27), (3, 5, 27), (3, 9, 27)... try out all the possible combinations until you reach the correct one.

It is still a lot of work, but not as much trying all the combinations without narrowing them down in this manner.

The moment you reach the correct combination of the possibilities, the lock will open. If you do not want to get into this mathematical procedure, you can explore shimming, which is another suitable technique for cracking a combination lock that has a shackle (we'll look at this in a few).

- *Multiple dial lock*

Multiple dial locks are simple combination locks used in low-level security applications. These locks are common in bicycle locks, briefcases, and travel bags and are very prone to cracking.

Figure 34 image credit Shutterstock

This combination lock, as shown above, has four dials with notches cut into each one of them and a pin with several teeth that hook onto the rotating dials securing the shackle.

Entering the correct code will align the notches on the dials with the pin's teeth to release the shackle, hence opening the lock. When you move the dials, the notches misalign with the pins, thus restraining the shackle and keeping the lock locked.

How to pick a multiple-dial padlock

Let's take an example of the multiple padlocks in image 4.14 above. This padlock doesn't use a key, so we shall not need any lock-picking tool. Let's see how we can crack the code to unlock the lock.

Tools: a multiple-dial lock and a rope.

- Apply pressure on the shackle

You can use your hand or the rope to apply pressure on the shackle.

Apply the pressure by pulling out the shackle using your hand or tie the rope on the shackle and pull. Using a rope is more advisable since you will need to apply pressure throughout the picking process.

To use the rope, tie it on the shackle and maybe on another firm object and pull the lock. This pressure will create friction on the dials, which is ideal for providing feedback during picking.

- Find the first dial

Here we will find the 'binding dial' (just to use a more familiar word by now). As you maintain the pressure, rotate each dial to feel the tension. Identify the hardest one to rotate of all the dials. This is your first dial.

- Rotate the dial to find its code

Once you have identified your first dial, rotate it until you hear an audible click. Rotate it again several rounds to the click. If you get the click on the same number on the dial, note the number down, as this is your first code.

- Find and set the subsequent dials

Try rotating the remaining dials to find your second dial as you maintain the pressure on the shackle. After finding it, rotate to the click and note the code after confirmation by several rotations.

Do the same with the rest of the codes until you determine the codes for all the dials. Remember to note down each code.

Once you have set your final dial, the codes will match the one you had solved, and the pins will have aligned with the pins' teeth, forcing the shackle to break loose and unlocking the lock.

- ***Shimming***

As the name suggests, shimming is a lock-picking technique in which you will use a tool called a shim. A shim is a thin metallic tool used to pick a lock by inserting it between the shackle and the body of a locked lock. This tool is very thin so that it can fit in through the narrow space left between the shackle and the body of a locked lock.

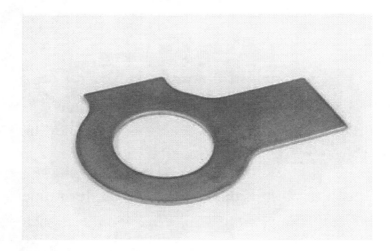

[34]**Figure 35 image credit Shutterstock**

This is how you get started with shimming:

- Examine your lock

First, check if your lock has enough space so the shim can fit in between the shackle and the body. Also, determine whether the lock you want to pick has a double or a single latch.

A single latch means the lock has a latch only on one side of the shackle, while a double latch means both shackles have latches. For double-latched locks, you will need to shim both shackles to pick them successfully.

Let's say our lock is double-latched and has sufficient space for the shim.

- Wrap the shim around the lock

Since our lock is double latched, wrap the shims on both sides. The u-shape side of your shim should be facing outwards as you wrap them

- Slide the shim into the lock

Slide the shim into the lock through the clearance between the shackle and the body of the lock. Push it gently as you twist it to ensure it goes as deep as possible without breaking. Do this to both the other shim on the other side of the shackle.

- Rotate the shim

Once the shim has reached the furthest end, gently rotate it to allow the part inside to approach the latch from one side.

Do this as gently as possible to avoid breaking the shim inside the lock.

This will disengage the latch from the shackle, thereby unlocking it. Do the same on the other side of the shackle. Once both sides of our double latched lock are done, the shackle will spring up open – you will have unlocked your lock successfully.

How to make a DIY Padlock shim

Losing your key is never planned for. This means that the probability of being locked out without any tool is very high. Ordering a shim may take quite some time which may not help save the situation. However, this does not mean you cannot access a shim to pick your lock. You can use easily accessible things to make your tool.

For this, all you will need is a soda or aluminum can and a pair of scissors, a knife, or a blade.

- Find aluminum can

You can find a can from your dust bin or if you don't have any, from the nearest shop or bar, pick a can of soda or beer. Empty the content as you ensure not to make ridges on the can to keep the aluminum sheet as smooth as possible.

After emptying the can, rinse out the residue using warm water.

- Cut off the top and bottom of the can

Use your knife or the blade to chop off the top and bottom of the can at the parts that border the body at either the bottom or the top.

To ensure that you make a fine cut, you may use the knife to create an opening and then use your pair of scissors to cut it around.

- Cut a vertical line

Once you have removed the top and the bottom, you will be left with an open cylinder. Using your pair of scissors for a smooth cut, make a vertical cut from top to bottom to open the cylinder into a rectangular metallic sheet.

As you make your cut, ensure that you make it along the seam of the can, and in case your can doesn't have a seam, try as much as possible to make a straight-line cut.

Up to this point, you will have reduced the can into a flat rectangular metallic sheet which is much easier to work with. Trim the edges to remove any rough cuts you may have made in the process. Also, rinse it with warm soapy water if it still has traces of soda. Rinse your cutting tools as well.

- Shape the metallic sheet into a shim

Following the size of a can, your rectangular sheet must be bigger than the size you need to make a single shim. Probably twice as big or even more. So, before you make a shim out of it, cut the metallic sheet into two equal rectangles. This will give you a sizable piece for a single shim.

From the two sheets, make an M shape cut.

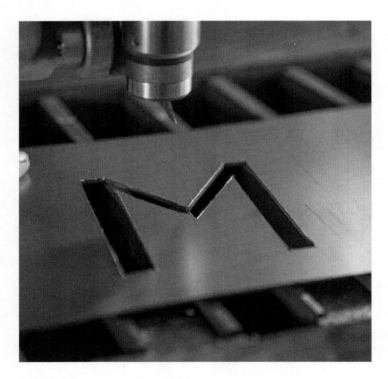

35Figure 36 Image Credit Imagefx

Having these marks makes it easier to make a good M shape cut. Cut along the lines of the M

Ensure your cut is as smooth as possible, and make the hump rounded and not pointy.

In the marked sheet, there are two lines on the uncut part of the sheet above the M shape cut. Fold that uncut part into two, following the line dividing the M into two. This will form the handle of the shim.

After that, fold the flaps on both sides of the M shape and cut upwards to wrap around the upper part that you just folded. Grip the handle as hard as possible using pliers.

After folding the two flips, you will have a T-shaped metal piece. Smooth the shim by wrapping it around the marker pen, as shown below, to take the shape of a shim pick finally.

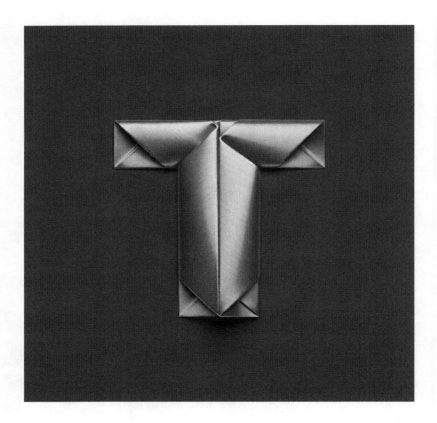

36Figure 37 image credit Imagefx

Lever Locks

After pin tumbler locks, lever locks are the most commonly used locks. They are mostly used in commercial buildings and homes' interior doors.

Lever locks use levers of different heights that move up and down to lock and unlock the door.

76

[37]**Figure 38 image credit iStock**

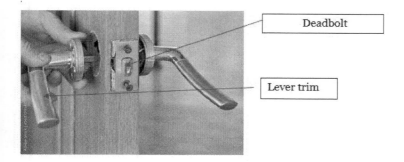

Deadbolt

Lever trim

[38]**Figure 39 image credit Stock Adobe**

These locks have between three to five levers. When you are opening the lock, the key moves the levers to their appropriate height disengaging the bolt to unlock the door.

How to pick lever locks

Let us now look at how to pick a five-lever lock.

Tools: a tension tool and a hook pick

For you to pick lever locks, you will need to raise each of the five levers to release the bolt to open the lock.

- Find out the number of levers the lock has

In our case here, we already know that we will pick a five-lever lock, but this step is crucial when you want to pick a lock that you do not know its number of levers.

To determine the number of levers, insert the hook into the lock at the top of the keyhole, then scroll it around to feel the number of levers.

- Insert the tension wrench

After knowing the lock's number of levers, withdraw the hook and insert the tension wrench into the lock at the bottom of the keyway. Push the wrench until it reaches the end of the keyhole, and move it around until you feel a notch/cut in the bolt.

Once you find the notch, turn the tension wrench in the direction the lock opens (it can be in either a clockwise or anticlockwise direction) until it stops moving further. Hold

78

the tension wrench in that place, applying moderate tension to it.

- Insert the hook

As you maintain the tension on the wrench, insert the hook at the top of the keyway, and try pushing the levers up using the hook to identify the stiffer lever to move.

After you have found the more rigid lever, still maintaining the tension on the wrench, lift this lever until you feel the bolt move a bit and the lever doesn't move any further. This will be the exact height this lever should move to unlock the lock.

- Set the subsequent levers

Once you have successfully set the first lever, test the remaining levers to find the next stiffer lever to move, maintaining the tension on the wrench. Lift that lever up to where you feel the bolt move, and the lever stops moving up.

Do the same to all the remaining levers until you set all of them successfully.

After lifting all the levers, turn the wrench to turn the bolt, which will unlock the lock.

Car Locks

Just like in all the other locks, car locks are made in a way that they resist attempts to unlock them without their keys. Most car locks are made with types of locks like pin tumblers, wafer locks, and other lock mechanisms. This means that the techniques and tools used to unlock them vary with the car model.

In picking car locks, we shall consider factors like the model of the car and manufacturing dates. This is because cars manufactured later than 1992 have more components incorporated in their lock systems. For cars manufactured before 1992, using lock picks and applying the basic lock-picking techniques should be your first option.

Due to the continuous growth of technology, just as cars are upgraded over time, their locks also improve daily. This means that picking these locks gets complicated every day.

How to pick car locks

There are various techniques you can employ to open a car lock:-

1. Unlocking using a Slim Jim

A slim jim is a thin metallic strip made with a notch on one end and a handle on the other end.

39Figure 40 image credit iStock

This tool is used in picking doors of a manual car door. To pick the car lock using this technique, you will need a small wedge and a slim jim.

81

Since we will pick a manual car door, the door must have an upright lock that protrudes from the door outwards.

⁴⁰Figure 41 image credit iStock

Procedure:

- On the passengers' door

We will be picking the lock on the passenger's door. Locksmiths recommend passengers' doors so that just in case of any damage on the lock, it will be on the door you do not use most frequently.

- Insert the wedge

Insert your wedge on the passenger's door in between the window and the weather strip (the rubber strip running between the door and the window). The wedge will create a space between which you will use to insert the slim jim.

Ensure that you use a wedge that is specifically for car doors.

82

Ensure that you insert the wedge just by the car lock. Do not insert it so far away from the lock.

- Insert the slim jim

Once you have the space, insert the slim jim into the door through that space. As you insert it, ensure that the notch is facing the lock. Push the slim jim inside the door towards the keyhole. Be gentle and slow as you insert the slim jim so as not to ruin things and damage the door.

Once your slim jim is inside the door, move it towards the keyhole until you feel it has gotten hold of the lock.

[41]**Figure 42 Image Credit Imagefx**

Note that the door has several components that the notch can get hold of, so watch the protruded lock mechanism, the one shown above. When the slim jim gets hold of the lock system from inside the door, you will see the protruded lock mechanism making some movements.

Try to move the slim jim side by side, and if the lock mechanism makes the same movements, then your tool is holding the right components.

- Pull the slim jim upwards

Once you are certain that the slim jim is holding the lock component, pull it upwards until the door unlocks. The door will open freely. Withdraw the slim jim and the wedge once you open the door. Do it gently to ensure that you do not cause unnecessary damage.

1. **Picking a car door using a screwdriver and a metallic rod with a hook**

Using a screwdriver and a hooked metallic rod works best for car doors with lock mechanisms like the one below.

⁴²Figure 43 image credit Freepik

You can use this technique to unlock other car doors, but it will work much easier and faster for such kinds of car doors.

Tools: a screwdriver and a metallic rod with a hood on one end

Procedure:

1. Insert the screwdriver between the door and the car body, then tilt the screwdriver as if you want to force the door open. This will create a space that you will use to insert the metallic rod.

2. Insert the hook end of the metallic rod inside the car through the space you created above.

3. Holding on to the screwdriver to maintain the space, try to move the hook until it reaches the lock mechanism.

4. Once you reach the door mechanism, ensure the hook takes hold of it and pull several times until it unlocks.

2. *Picking a car lock using a bobby pin*

1. Insert the bobby pin lock pick into the lock through the keyway and move it up and down, applying moderate tension.

2. As you move the bobby pin, move the barrel simultaneously to initiate a key turning in the car door lock.

3. After you find the correct combination, you can turn the lock quickly to unlock it.

Picking a car lock is not limited to the three techniques discussed above. Since car locks are not standardized, we cannot be restricted to only these three techniques. There are more techniques you can explore to have vast knowledge and options to save yourself from such a frustrating situation.

Having gone through the techniques and how to apply them to various locks, let us now look at some lock-picking mistakes that every beginner must try as much as possible to avoid.

Chapter 5: Lock-Picking Mistakes to Avoid

Making mistakes is the beauty and the accelerator of learning. As a beginner, there are mistakes that you must avoid if you want to learn lock-picking better. However, some errors will derail your learning process instead of helping you learn faster. In this chapter, you will learn the typical mistakes beginners make that you must avoid as much as possible if you want to learn lock picking successfully.

Below are some of the mistakes you must avoid as a learner:

1. Solely focusing on a single lock-picking technique

As a beginner, the moment you first pick your first lock successfully is indeed exciting. You will get more excited the day you learn how to manipulate a lock faster. Most beginners and even professional lock pickers tend to focus on one technique they feel works best for them. A perfect example is raking, the most popular technique since it's a faster technique.

Focusing on your favorite technique will surely make your operation very efficient using the specific method. However, focusing on a single technique is not advisable since your

87

favorite technique cannot work on all locks. Being a pro in a single method will limit your operation. Yes, you may be able to pick a lock using other techniques, but remember, practice makes perfect. The more you ignore other techniques, the more they will be challenging to you.

To become a good picker, you need to equip yourself with as many techniques as possible so that you will be able to pick a variety of locks.

2. Practice using one lock over and over again

As a beginner, you should practice using different locks. When you repeatedly use the same lock, you will be a pro in picking that one. But remember that locks are not the same. Many types of locks are diverse in their mechanisms, meaning that applying the picking techniques must be precisely the same for all locks.

It is essential to note that locks have different modifications; even the same type of locks from different manufacturers are never the same.

For example, manufacturers A and B are producing pin tumbler locks. Manufacturer A makes their pin tumbler locks with additional anti-picking pins, while B doesn't. If you have only been practicing using locks with no anti-picking pins, you will think that you are now the master of picking all the pin tumbler locks. Picking locks manufactured by A with this extra security pin will be very challenging and frustrating. You must then have as wide exposure with different locks as possible.

3. Practice using complex locks to pick

As a beginner, it is only appropriate to start your practice with simple locks. Using simple locks will allow you to apply basic skills and easily pick locks.

Practicing with complex locks is good for challenging yourself, but not as a beginner. Continuous unsuccessful attempts to pick these locks can be discouraging and frustrating. You may even end up losing interest totally.

As well, always using simple locks to practice will stagnate your growth. To avoid losing interest and stagnation in your learning;

- *Create a plan:* Have a detailed plan on how you will proceed with your learning. Ensure that your plan is sequential, from starting with simple locks and learning a technique to advancing with time to more complex ones.

- *Have a break:* Learn to take a break whenever you get stuck in a process. Do not be too hard on yourself when you realize that the method you are learning is not working out at that time. So as not to get frustrated beyond repair, leave that method aside and return to the other ones you had practiced successfully. This will help motivate you.

4. Depending on transparent locks

Most beginners make the mistake of getting obsessed with transparent locks. Transparent locks are purposely meant to enable you to understand lock-picking concepts. You should never take these locks as your practicing lock.

Always remember that the actual locks you are learning to pick are never transparent. If you can only pick locks that you can see their internal components, then you will fail at the actual job.

5. Not practicing regularly

It is said, "Practice makes perfect." For you to perfect picking locks, you must practice regularly. Practicing regularly will allow you to learn new ways of applying the techniques much better.

Not practicing will drag your learning pace, so ensure that you are consistent.

6. Applying excess tension

Always ensure that you apply appropriate tension on your lock. As we have seen in most lock-picking techniques, tension is critical. How you apply tension on the lock you are picking determines whether you will succeed.

If you apply excess tension, for example, on the combination locks, the dials will be stiff to the extent that you cannot rotate any to crack the code. If you apply less tension, the dials will move freely, making identifying the dial you need to spin first challenging.

7. Purchasing low-quality tools

As you purchase your first lock-picking set of tools, ensure you get a good quality set. High-quality lock-picking tools might seem too expensive, but rest assured that cheap and low-quality pick sets are more costly in the long run.

Low-quality tools are cheap, but they can break easily or bend when in use, making them ineffective. As a beginner, it is good to have tools that will give you an easy time learning without any inconveniences.

This does not mean you need to spend a massive amount of money on purchasing tools, but be keen to ensure that you get good quality that will serve you well as you buy your tools.

Conclusion

Lock picking is a very easy-to-learn technique that can save you big. This book contains the ideal procedures for anyone who would like to know how to pick a lock. I have written this book in the most straightforward language that anyone can follow and learn independently without being taken through it. This book is ideal for first-timers who know nothing about lock picking and intermediates looking for a resource to sharpen their skills.

Losing your key is always an uncertainty. This frustrating experience rarely finds you ready with the most appropriate tools unless you are a professional locksmith. Therefore, I advise that you take the process of making your own tools out of whatever you can easily find seriously. This will save you the inconveniences, the cost, and the time of finding the tools.

And now that you have become a pro in lock picking, do not forget to be ethical by only picking your own locks; if you have to pick anybody's lock, only do that with their permission.

I hope that this book has been of great help; good luck!

PS: I'd like your feedback. If you are happy with this book, please leave a review on Amazon.

Please leave a review for this book on Amazon by visiting the page below:

https://amzn.to/2VMR5qr

---

[1] https://media.istockphoto.com/id/2064090187/photo/small-parts-of-deadbolt-lock-to-protect-security-safety-on-door-window-house-incomplete-many.webp?b=1&s=612x612&w=0&k=20&c=uL6RN9ncKp6q6ozCOnES1edAccVymSCjw6GN8Zmbnnc=

[2] https://www.shutterstock.com/image-photo/stainless-steel-bidirectional-spring-hinge-260nw-2493365733.jpg

[3] https://www.istockphoto.com/photo/small-parts-of-deadbolt-lock-to-protect-security-safety-on-door-window-house-gm2017536677-561203567?utm_medium=organic&utm_source=google&utm_campaign=iptcurl

[4] https://www.shutterstock.com/image-illustration/steel-door-latch-barrel-bolt-600nw-283155806.jpg

5 https://www.shutterstock.com/image-illustration/3d-iilustration-door-lock-strike-260nw-2327912707.jpg

6 https://www.vectorstock.com/royalty-free-vector/realistic-door-handles-different-metal-furniture-vector-44371323

7 https://www.shutterstock.com/image-illustration/realistic-3d-render-lock-picks-260nw-2087627035.jpg

8 https://www.shutterstock.com/image-illustration/realistic-3d-render-lock-picks-260nw-2087627035.jpg

9 https://www.shutterstock.com/image-illustration/realistic-3d-render-lock-picks-260nw-2087627035.jpg

10 https://www.shutterstock.com/image-illustration/realistic-3d-render-lock-picks-260nw-2087627035.jpg

11 https://aitestkitchen.withgoogle.com/tools/image-fx/1uks8ksqog000

12 https://aitestkitchen.withgoogle.com/tools/image-fx/49pged4ft0000

13 https://www.shutterstock.com/image-photo/lock-picking-tension-wrench-inserted-260nw-1793736949.jpg

14 https://www.shutterstock.com/image-illustration/realistic-3d-render-lock-picks-260nw-2087627035.jpg

15   https://www.shutterstock.com/image-vector/lock-pick-gun-vector-icon-260nw-2375340193.jpg

16   https://thumbs.dreamstime.com/b/lock-pick-several-lockpicking-to-open-door-84366746.jpg

17   https://www.shutterstock.com/image-photo/closeup-shiny-metal-shim-on-260nw-1624489009.jpg

18   https://www.istockphoto.com/photo/lock-picking-an-unlocked-padlock-with-a-paperclip-overhead-view-gm503678558-82679021?utm_medium=organic&utm_source=google&utm_campaign=iptcurl

19 https://aitestkitchen.withgoogle.com/tools/image-fx/0m68c304c0000

20 https://aitestkitchen.withgoogle.com/tools/image-fx/7e99aqka4g000

21   https://www.alamy.com/stock-photo-picking-a-pin-tumbler-lock-1-86351714.html

22 https://stock.adobe.com/ke/images/spring-compressed-cylinder-lock-with-pins-exposed-various-tools-and-parts-shown-in-the-background/443857817?start-checkout=1&content-id=443857817

23   https://encrypted-tbn0.gstatic.com/images?q=tbn:ANd9GcTrk4zn-Q1dNonFoaltTOItcQMZeSft_9v1dw&s

[24] https://www.istockphoto.com/photo/pin-tumbler-of-cylinder-lock-internal-mechanism-and-set-of-keys-gm967560994-263914367?utm_medium=organic&utm_source=google&utm_campaign=iptcurl

[25] https://www.shutterstock.com/image-photo/tubular-lock-payment-terminals-slot-260nw-536696146.jpg

[26] https://www.istockphoto.com/photo/padlock-with-key-open-and-closed-gm176113864-10649892?utm_medium=organic&utm_source=google&utm_campaign=iptcurl

[27] https://thumbs.dreamstime.com/b/transparent-padlock-show-mechanics-how-to-lock-blue-color-96848805.jpg

[28] https://www.shutterstock.com/image-photo/new-waterproof-padlock-keys-260nw-1404391022.jpg

[29] https://thumbs.dreamstime.com/b/hanging-locked-metal-shining-padlock-closed-iron-shackle-icon-secure-private-access-realistic-flat-cartoon-vector-226182059.jpg

[30] https://thumbs.dreamstime.com/b/padlock-23166850.jpg

31   https://www.istockphoto.com/photo/padlock-on-cargo-container-gm594065234-101897101?utm_medium=organic&utm_source=google&utm_campaign=iptcurl

32 https://www.shutterstock.com/image-vector/rotary-combination-lock-safe-locking-260nw-86652352.jpg

33   https://www.shutterstock.com/image-vector/combination-padlock-realistic-metal-vector-260nw-621347417.jpg

34   https://www.shutterstock.com/image-photo/closeup-shiny-metal-shim-on-260nw-1624489009.jpg

35 https://aitestkitchen.withgoogle.com/tools/image-fx/6dar8hdrt0000

36 https://aitestkitchen.withgoogle.com/tools/image-fx/603q4na4b0000

37   https://www.istockphoto.com/photo/nickel-plated-closet-door-lever-gm1302342063-394114712?utm_medium=organic&utm_source=google&utm_campaign=iptcurl

38

https://as2.ftcdn.net/v2/jpg/05/68/75/99/1000_F_568759948_FsJpFy3N79r7ZOacS3KqkbqfirwfKBUU.jpg

39   https://www.istockphoto.com/photo/automobile-thief-gm177441750-21326062?utm_medium=organic&utm_source=google&utm_campaign=iptcurl

40   https://www.istockphoto.com/video/car-door-lock-in-motion-close-up-hd-gm472681461-11468814?utm_medium=organic&utm_source=google&utm_campaign=iptcurl

41 https://aitestkitchen.withgoogle.com/tools/image-fx/16cdtmavv0000

42   https://www.freepik.com/premium-photo/car-door-lock-lever-inside-driver-place_3454906.htm

Made in United States
Orlando, FL
07 December 2024

55155037R00054